World Book, Inc.
180 North LaSalle Street
Suite 900
Chicago, Illinois 60601
USA

For information about other "True or False?" titles, as well as other World Book print and digital publications, please go to www.worldbook.com.

For information about other World Book publications, call 1-800-WORLDBK (967-5325).

For information about sales to schools and libraries, call 1-800-975-3250 (United States) or 1-800-837-5365 (Canada).

Library of Congress Cataloging-in-Publication Data for this volume has been applied for.

True or False?
ISBN: 978-0-7166-3725-7 (set, hc.)

Video Games
ISBN: 978-0-7166-3735-6 (hc.)

Also available as:
ISBN: 978-0-7166-3745-5 (e-book)

Printed in China by Shenzhen Wing King Tong Paper Products Co., Ltd., Shenzhen, Guangdong
1st printing July 2018

Staff

Executive Committee

President
Jim O'Rourke

Vice President and
Editor in Chief
Paul A. Kobasa

Vice President, Finance
Donald D. Keller

Vice President, Marketing
Jean Lin

Vice President, International
Maksim Rutenberg

Vice President, Technology
Jason Dole

Director, Human Resources
Bev Ecker

Editorial

Director, New Print
Tom Evans

Writer
Will Adams

Editor
Grace Guibert

Librarian
S. Thomas Richardson

Manager, Contracts and
Compliance
(Rights and Permissions)
Loranne K. Shields

Manager, Indexing Services
David Pofelski

Digital

Director, Digital Product
Development
Erika Meller

Digital Product Manager
Jonathan Wills

Manufacturing/Production

Manufacturing Manager
Anne Fritzinger

Production Specialist
Curley Hunter

Proofreader
Nathalie Strassheim

Graphics and Design

Senior Art Director
Tom Evans

Senior Visual
Communications Designer
Melanie Bender

Senior Designer
Isaiah Sheppard

Media Editor
Rosalia Bledsoe

TRUE OR FALSE?

VIDEO GAMES

WORLD BOOK

www.worldbook.com

TRUE OR FALSE?

The first chess-playing program
didn't run on a computer.

In 1951, the English mathematician Alan Turing wrote out a simple chess program on paper. He tried it out against a bad chess player, but the program still lost. Today, computer programs can beat even the best human players of many board and card games, such as chess, go, and poker.

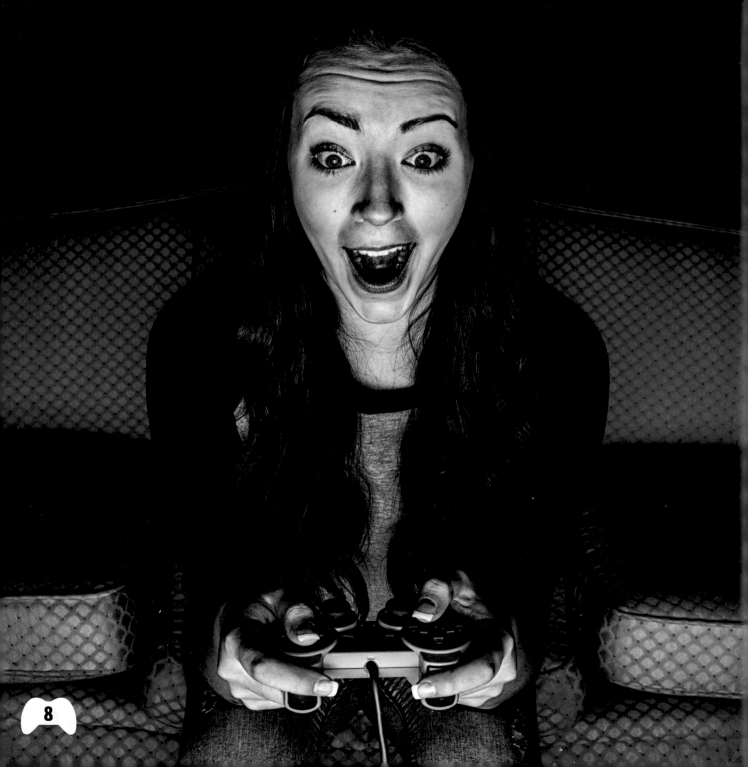

TRUE OR FALSE?

Great games have always been addictive.

One of the first computer games was banned from some universities because it was wasting people's time and hogging computer resources. The game *Spacewar!* was created in 1961 to show the power of a new computer a laboratory had just bought. It was so popular that the lab had to ban people from playing it during work hours!

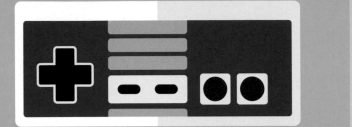

Nintendo, Sony, and Microsoft have all been making video game *consoles* since the 1970's. A console is a special computer made for playing games.

13

14

Many different companies made video game consoles in the early days of video games, such as Sega, Atari, and Magnavox. But Microsoft is new to the console business, with its first Xbox console released in 2001.

TRUE OR FALSE?

Parents didn't like early video games because they kept kids from hanging out together.

Parents didn't like early video games because kids left the house to play them! From the mid-1970's to the mid-1990's, kids and teens gathered at places called *arcades* to play the new games, where parents were not welcome. Such arcade games were built into large cabinets and cost small amounts of money to play.

19

TRUE OR FALSE?

The first successful arcade game, called *Pong,* was so popular that the machines kept jamming with coins.

The game was very popular, but the story of it jamming with coins was likely made up by the company that made the game—Atari—to promote it.

TRUE OR FALSE?

Nintendo was founded in 1980.
Its founders saw how popular
game consoles were, and they
wanted to get into the business.

Nintendo was founded in 1889 to make traditional Japanese playing cards called *hanafuda*. The company branched out into other toys and electronic games in the 1960's, eventually releasing the famous Nintendo Entertainment System (called Famicom, in Japan) in the 1980's. Nintendo sticks to its roots: it still sells *hanafuda* cards in Japan!

TRUE OR FALSE?

There was an electronic game
about teeth brushing.

TRUE!

Plaque Attack was a 1983 computer game where players had to stop plaque monsters from rotting teeth.

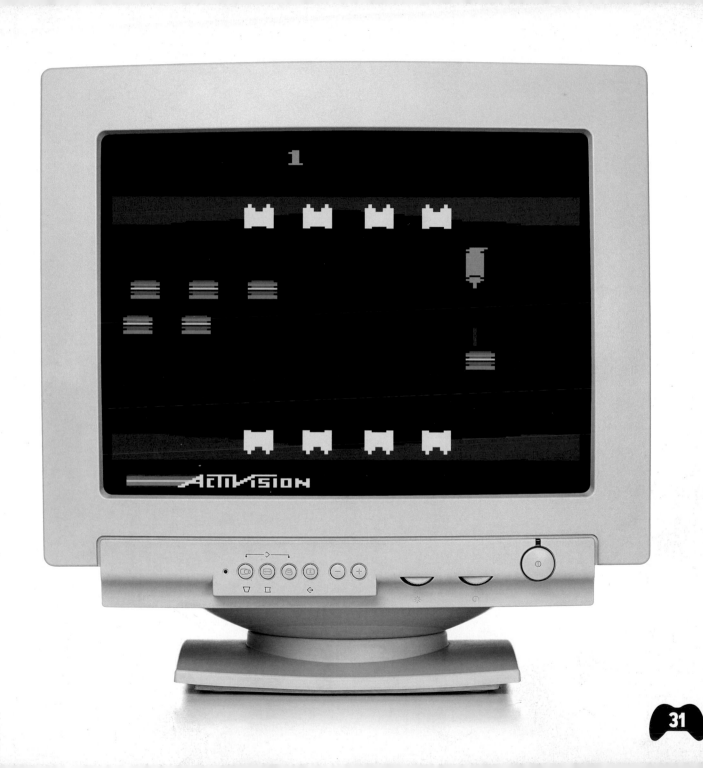

TRUE OR FALSE?

One video game was so bad that its maker buried all unsold copies in a landfill.

The company Atari buried their unsold copies of *E.T. the Extra-Terrestrial* in 1983. It was a very difficult and frustrating game. The failure of *E.T.* marked the beginning of a crash in home video game sales in North America. Bad games and too many consoles caused people to stop buying video games. Console and game sales shrunk 97% from 1983 to 1985.

The Atari Mindlink would have let you play video games with brain waves as early as the mid-1980's, but the government shut it down.

36

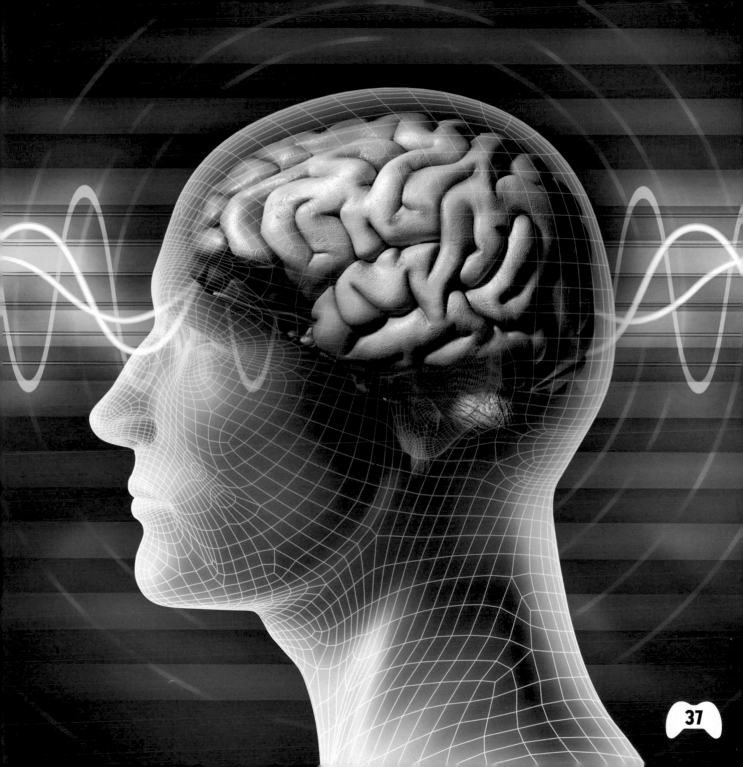

The electronic game company Atari was testing a device called the Mindlink. But it really picked up tiny muscle movements in the player's forehead to control a game. It was the North American console crash of the mid-1980's, not the government, that caused Atari to stop working on it.

MindLink System

20000

The ATAF

It works

...ables you to control your Atari game
...moving, seemingly by magic!
...o interact with every individual's

39

TRUE OR FALSE?

Before Nintendo's famous character Mario was a princess-saving plumber, he was a carpenter named Jumpman.

Jumpman the carpenter made his first appearance in *Donkey Kong* in 1981. When he was to star in his own game, the designers decided to make him a plumber since much of the action took place underground. He was renamed Mario after the owner of a U.S. warehouse that Nintendo rented.

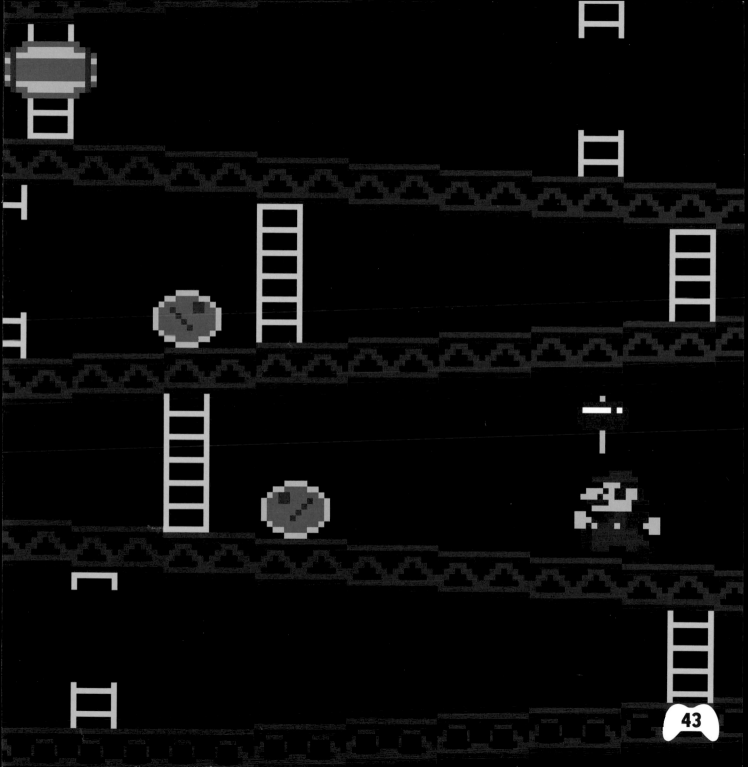

The first video game to tell a story was the adventure game *The Legend of Zelda*, released in 1986.

In the 1970's, American computer programmer William Crowther created *Colossal Cave Adventure.* It was a *text-based adventure game,* a type of computer game played by reading text and typing out commands.

TRUE OR FALSE?

The popular simulation franchise SimCity got its start as a government project on how to design better cities.

49

The game's creator, Will Wright, was working on building islands to attack for a different game. He found creating the islands more fun than playing the original game, so he decided to turn it into a city-planning game. *SimCity* was released in 1989.

TRUE OR FALSE?

The *gene* (part of a cell that determines which traits living things get from their parents) that makes animals run fast is called *Sonic hedgehog* in honor of Sega's speedy blue mascot.

But Sonic has, in fact, lent his name to a very important gene! *Sonic hedgehog* (or SHH) controls many parts of proper body development in animals with backbones—including humans!

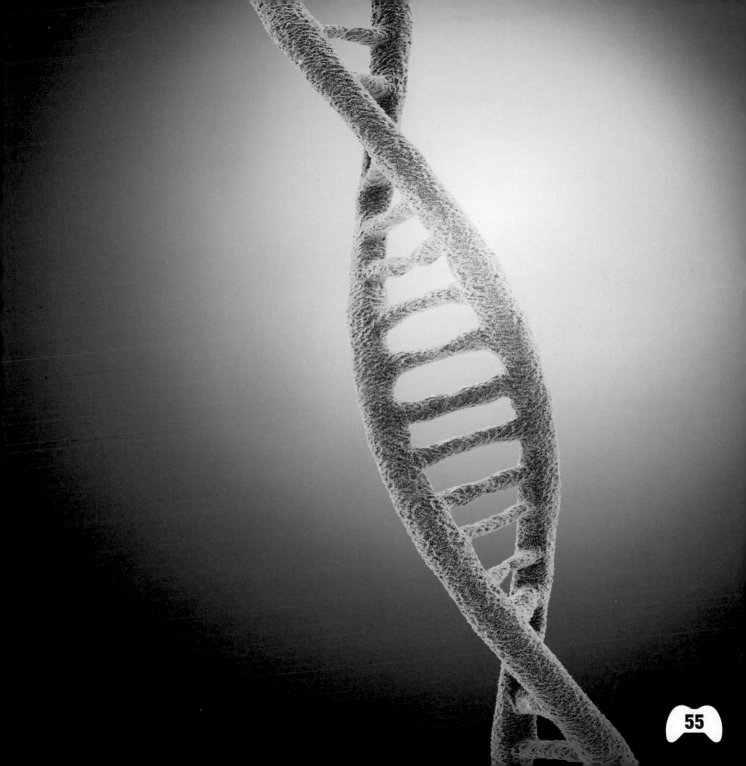

TRUE OR FALSE?

One of the best-rated computer games of the early 1990's ended with a glitch.

TRUE!

The sci-fi combat simulator *Wing Commander* would crash and display an error message every time the player quit the game. The programmers couldn't figure out what was causing the problem. So they just edited the error text to say, "Thank you for playing Wing Commander!"

TRUE OR FALSE?

The famous computer game studio Blizzard Entertainment got its name because its workers used to shovel snow to make extra money.

FALSE!

The company was first called Silicon and Synapse. After a number of name changes, the founders picked "blizzard" from a dictionary. The company went on to create the StarCraft, Warcraft, and Overwatch game franchises.

TRUE OR FALSE?

Electronic games had no rating system at first. But as games became more violent, the U.S. government thought they should be rated.

TRUE!

Concerns about the nature of the content in some games, such as the violent fighting game *Mortal Kombat,* forced the gaming industry to create the Entertainment Software Rating Board (ESRB) in 1994 to rate the content of new games.

67

TRUE OR FALSE?

The creator of Pokémon, Satoshi Tajiri, drew inspiration from sitting at home.

69

As a child, Tajiri loved nature and collected bugs. The thrill and mystery of discovering new bugs inspired him to create Pokémon.

TRUE OR FALSE?

People play electronic games professionally—as a job!

TRUE!

The professional playing of electronic games is known as electronic sports, or e-sports. One e-sport tournament handed out over $24 million in prize money!

TRUE OR FALSE?

Most people play electronic games
on video game consoles.

Since the late 2000's, most people play games on smartphones. They work for people who don't have time to play games on consoles or computers, or who can't afford such a setup. Such apps as *Angry Birds, Candy Crush Saga,* and *Clash of Clans* are some of the most popular electronic games of all time.

TRUE OR FALSE?

Some popular games today came from changes that players made to existing games. These new games are called action real-time strategy games.

Sykkuno
15

+29xp

jaybird02
10

mendoliumnomnom
13

Benjamander
15

29   167   70

Q   W   E   R   D   F   B

1190 / 1938   +3.3

81

TRUE!

Players made modifications ("mods" for short) to other games, such as *StarCraft* and *Warcraft III.* These modded games featured small teams of characters with special abilities. Today, action real-time strategy games are among the most popular games for e-sports.

Some video games are great exercise.

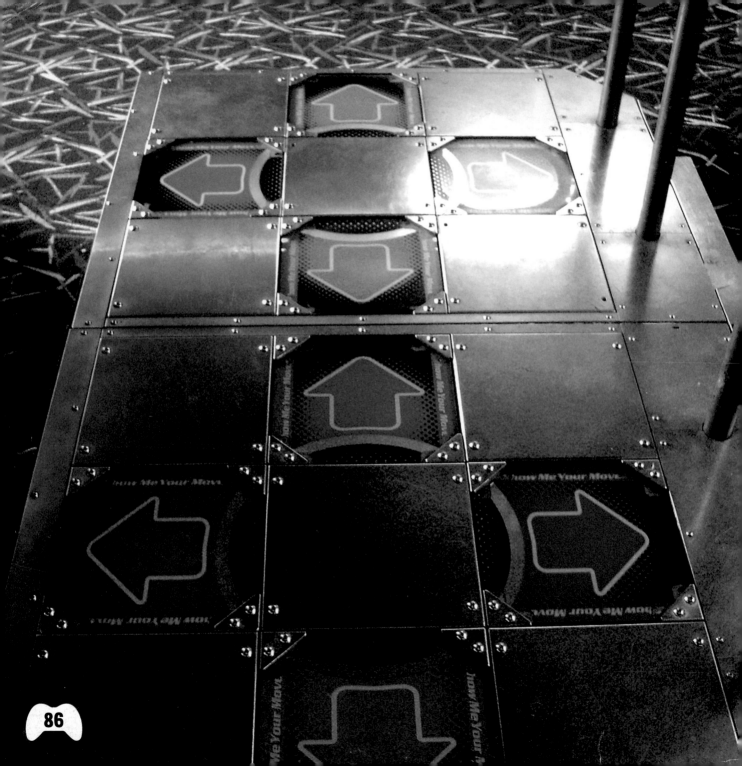

A few arcade and video games, such as the Dance Dance Revolution series, have special mats or platforms on which players press buttons with their feet, making gameplay a real workout! But most video games aren't good exercise—make sure you put down the controller and go outside!

87

World of Warcraft is the largest massively multiplayer online role-playing game (MMORPG), with millions of players interacting in a huge online world.

FALSE!

World of Warcraft is the largest MMORPG in terms of number of players, but they are divided into similar worlds of approximately 5,000-15,000 players each. But the science-fiction MMORPG *Eve Online* takes place in single world. Tens of thousands of players play together at the same time.

DID YOU KNOW...

Tomohiro Nishikado, the creator of the famous arcade game *Space Invaders*, is terrible at it!

The most **famous cheat code,** called the Konami code for the company that created it, is Up Up Down Down Left Right Left Right B A. Try it out in your favorite game and see what happens!

GAME OVER

The first **U.S. football game** in what is now the Madden NFL series was released **in 1988.**

A computer called **Deep Blue** was the first to beat a chess world champion. It defeated Garry Kasparov in 1997.

The appearance of the iconic arcade game character **Pac-Man** was inspired by the shape of a pizza with a piece missing.

Index

Acknowledgments

Cover: © Elys Art/Shutterstock; © Dean Drobot, Shutterstock; © Mary Super Studio/Shutterstock

5-8   © Shutterstock

11   © Steve Russell

12-17   © Shutterstock

19   © Mike Goldwater, Alamy Images

20   © Maulsmash/Shutterstock

23   © Paul Simpson

25   © Waraporn Chokchaiworarat, Shutterstock

27   © Miyuki Satake, Dreamstime

28   ©Tanya_MTV/Shutterstock

31   © Rangizzz/Shutterstock; © Activision

32-33   Digital Game Museum (licensed under CC BY 2.0)

34-35   © Vchal/Shutterstock; *E.T. the Extra-Terrestrial* © Universal Pictures

37   © Andrea Danti, Shutterstock

39   © Charlie Knoblock, AP Photo

40   *Super Mario Bros.*® is a registered trademark of Nintendo; © Shutterstock

43   *Donkey Kong*® is a registered trademark of Nintendo

44   *The Legend of Zelda*® is a registered trademark of Nintendo

47   © ClassicStock/SuperStock; © Microsoft

49   © 927 Creation/Shutterstock

51   WORLD BOOK photo; © Maxis

53   *Sonic the Hedgehog*® is a registered trademark of Sega

55   © Nata-Lia/Shutterstock

56-59   © Origin Systems

60-61   © Foto Duets/Shutterstock

62-63   *World of Warcraft*® is a registered trademark of Blizzard Entertainment

65   © 4zevar/Shutterstock; © Midway Games' Chicago

67   © Entertainment Software Rating Board

68   © Shutterstock

71   *Pokémon* is a registered trademark of Nintendo; © Enchanted Fairy/Shutterstock

72-79   © Shutterstock

81   *League of Legends*® is a registered trademark of Riot Games

83   *StarCraft*® is a registered trademark of Blizzard Entertainment

84   Michael Ocampo (licensed under CC BY 2.0)

86   AeronPrometheus (licensed under CC BY-SA 4.0)

88-89   © Pe3k/Shutterstock

90-91   *Eve Online*® is a registered trademark of CCP Games

92-93   © Shutterstock